A Cup of Hope

31 DAILY READINGS TO REFRESH YOUR SOUL

Kim Crabill

BroadStreet
PUBLISHING

BroadStreet Publishing Group, LLC
Racine, Wisconsin, USA
BroadStreetPublishing.com

A Cup of Hope: 31 DAILY READINGS TO REFRESH YOUR SOUL

ISBN-13: 978-1-4245-5319-8 (softcover)
ISBN-13: 978-1-4245-5362-4 (e-book)

Stock or custom editions of BroadStreet Publishing titles may be purchased in bulk for educational, business, ministry, fundraising, or sales promotional use. For information, please e-mail info@broadstreetpublishing.com.

Cover design by Chris Garborg, GarborgDesign.com
Interior design by Katherine Lloyd, theDESKonline.com

Printed in the United States of America
16 17 18 19 20 5 4 3 2 1

To every worried, weighed-down woman
who thirsts for a cup of hope.

Day 1

Open my eyes that I may see
wonderful things.

—*Psalm 119:18*

My husband, Lee, and I were returning home from my mother's funeral service. The storm outside our car fit the turmoil within me. Finally, out of view of all the attendees, I gave way to tears.

Lee's voice broke through my wall of emotion. "Kim, open your eyes! You are not going to believe this!" His enthusiasm angered me. Couldn't he see I was grieving? Yet he persisted. "Kim, please, just for a minute—please, look up!"

Relenting, I opened my eyes. Dark skies had given way to light. The thunder had silenced, the lightning halted. And stretched across the horizon was the most beautiful rainbow I had ever seen.

I was immediately reminded of another rainbow given as a symbol of promise (Genesis 9:8–17). And in that moment of terrible pain, I knew I would find hope again. It took time, and a lot of relapses, before I was truly ready to "look up." But as I focused more and more, little by little, on the Source of all hope, I found a life that exceeded anything I could have imagined.

Have you lost sight of hope? Have the burdens of the past, the worries of the present, or the fear of the future dragged you so low that you can't imagine ever looking up again? I speak from experience: hope *will* return. But probably not in one mighty whoosh. More likely, it will return, as mine did, in tiny daily bits. And so I share with you these tiny daily readings. I pray they will help you, one day at a time, to open your eyes again, look up, and see the abundance in store for you through the Giver of hope.

Day 1

Dear Father, You know the hurt I bear, the burdens I carry. Please begin to fill me with fresh hope as I take a little time each day to look up at You. I echo the prayer in today's Bible verse: Open my eyes to see wonderful things. Open my eyes to hope. Amen.

Day 2

The Spirit in you is far stronger
than anything in the world.
—1 John 4:4 MSG

*Y*ou know what makes me feel helpless? A flat tire. Or a box of metal pieces and tires that are supposed to become a bicycle. Talk about stress! But aren't we modern women able to handle *anything*?

As you've guessed, this is about more than flat tires and bicycles. Has anyone ever told you, "God will not give you more than you can handle"? Friend, let me tell you: nowhere does God promise that life will not be more than we—Wonder Women that we are—can navigate. What He does say is that no matter what comes our way, He is in control. *He* can handle it. Believe 1 John 4:4—God is greater than anything in this world, including whatever you are facing that is beyond your understanding or capacity. Find hope today in knowing it's OK to feel helpless. But don't give in to feeling hopeless.

Dear Father, thank You for reminding me that though I'm often helpless on my own, I'm not without help. You are my help in trouble and joy. Because of that truth, I'm going to make "helpless but not hopeless" my new motto. Amen.

Day 3

Against all hope,
Abraham in hope believed.
—*Romans 4:18*

Abraham put his trust in God against all hope. He was old and his wife was barren, yet God had promised him offspring beyond count.

Where does that kind of hope come from? I believe Romans 4:21 holds the answer: Abraham was "fully persuaded that God had power to do what he had promised." Hope and faith are inseparable.

What seems dead to you today? Your marriage? Your dreams? What seems too large to conquer? Your depression? Your anger? A stubborn habit?

The same God who made Abraham a father

of nations offers His power to you today. Set aside your notion of what can't be done. Find hope today in knowing God is able (and eager!) to act powerfully in your life too. Against all hope, believe.

Dear Father, I'm tired of believing a lie—that there is no hope. Help me to be fully persuaded of Your power, like Abraham was. Show me that first, small step I can take toward You to restore my hope in the future. Amen.

Notes and Reflections

Day 4

"I am with you,"
declares the Lord.

—*Haggai 1:13*

School used to be a fairly safe place. But now we can't escape the news of widespread bullying.

As believers, we also have a bully (1 Peter 5:8). And he's not coming for our lunches; he's coming for our lives. He throws condescending remarks at us, reminds us of every mess-up, makes us feel small and insignificant … need I go on?

When school kids are bullied, their parents can't always be there. But Jesus goes everywhere you go today. He rides in the car with you, He sits in your meetings, He follows you into the ladies' room when your anxiety attack hits. So when your bully begins taunting you today, remind him who is by your side. Find hope today in knowing that at the mere whisper of Jesus's name, your bully must cease and desist.

Dear Father, thanks for reassuring me of Your constant presence. Today, when the bullying starts, I will cling to that truth. And I will look for someone else to encourage with Your words: "I am with you." Amen.

Day 5

Consider it pure joy . . . whenever you
face trials of many kinds, because you know
that the testing of your faith produces
perseverance . . . so that you may be mature
and complete, not lacking anything.

—*James 1:2–4*

When my boys were small, they dreaded their inoculations. So did I. How could I explain that the nurse was inflicting pain on them (that needle!) *with my permission*? What did they understand about big concepts like "future health and safety"? I'll never forget the accusation in those big, sad eyes.

Similarly, your heavenly Parent feels no pleasure in your pain. Yet He knows, as I knew with my boys, that the pain is not wasted. He is seeing to your spiritual health and well-being. Find hope today in knowing that, though you may not understand Him, you can trust Him.

Dear Father, You see what I cannot see. You know what I cannot know. You have a future for me in which I am mature, complete, and lacking nothing. I can't imagine that. I can't quite understand it. But my hope is in Your love for me, greater than that of any human parent. Amen.

Day 6

See what great love the Father
has lavished on us.

—*1 John 3:1*

"Jesus loves me, this I know." I used to sing that song while swinging on the front porch at night, serenading Daddy. Many times, I giggled in disbelief when Daddy told me that, as much as he loved me, there was someone who loved me even more. *No way*, I recall thinking. *How could that be?*

Now, as an adult, I know Daddy was right. He had planted truth in my heart: there is someone, Jesus, who does indeed love me more than anyone else can. And time and time again, when I've felt like a lonely little girl on a turbulent and terrifying journey, I have clung to that truth. Find hope today in knowing your Father's love is beyond any human love you can imagine.

Day 6

Dear Father, I cannot grasp how much You love me. Some days I deeply doubt Your love. That's how fragile my belief is. Strengthen my struggling heart today with a fresh experience of Your love. Let Your love become my pathway back to hope. Amen.

Notes and Reflections

Day 7

He will take great delight in you.

—*Zephaniah 3:17*

For years, nothing upset me more than if a relationship with a workmate, a ministry colleague, a good friend, or a family member seemed strained. I would worry, worry, worry about what I did wrong, how I might have disappointed that person, and what they might be saying about me. Sound familiar?

I've come to realize that to focus on what people are saying about me is to miss a much higher priority: a focus on what God has to say about me.

Let's refocus! Forgive what needs to be forgiven. Forget ugly words. Turn your back on negativity. Instead, run into the open arms of the One who says you are the apple of His eye, who delights in you, who calls you to purpose and significance today. Find hope today in knowing God is singing your praises!

Dear Father, thank You for delighting in me. Thank You for valuing me. I know I'll fight negativity from time to time—mine and others'. But now I know I can refocus away from negative words to Your uplifting words about how You view me. Amen.

Day 8

Whoever drinks the water
I give them will never thirst.

—John 4:14

Not too long ago, I found a dried-up sponge in my garage. It matched how I felt: sucked dry, brittle, and used up. But when I dropped that sponge in water, it was restored to usefulness. As good as new.

Jesus promises that something similar happens when we immerse ourselves in Him. Like living water, He fills us up, renews us, and satisfies us.

Has doing, doing, doing and working, working, working drained you of hope that you'll ever feel refreshed again? Make like a sponge and get wet! Pause to read a psalm. Listen to worship music as you make the kids' lunches. Sing to God in the car instead of muttering at the latest news. As you unload the dishwasher, praise God for one of His attributes with each glass, plate, and fork you put away. Find hope today as you soak in the living water of worship.

Dear Father, I want buckets of Your living water! I was starting to think I just had to live with this dried-up feeling. You have given me renewed hope that as I immerse myself in Your presence, I will learn what it means to never thirst again. What a promise! Amen.

Day 9

> You meant evil against me,
> but God meant it for good in order
> to bring about this present result.
> —*Genesis 50:20 NASB*

J oseph was one of the good guys. So where in
the world was God during those dark nights
in the pit, or when Joseph was being falsely ac-
cused? Only when you get to the end of Joseph's
story can you say, "Wow, God really did have a
plan!" Good thing Joseph never gave up, right?

We never really know what God is up to. But
we know He promises that all things are working for the good of those who love Him (Romans
8:28). And we know He promises never to leave
us as these plans slowly unfold. So what will we
choose to believe, even if we can't see a hope-
ful ending? Find hope today in knowing that

Day 9

whatever your current struggle, one day you will be exactly where you need to be.

Dear Father, thank You for this perspective. What I'm going through isn't easy, but I can see now that, like Joseph, I may be blazing a trail of hope for someone else. Give me strength to place my hope in Your promises, not in my circumstances. Amen.

Notes and Reflections

Day 10

We can comfort those in
any trouble with the comfort we
ourselves receive from God.

—*2 Corinthians 1:4*

My garage is packed, my pantry is filled, and my closet overflows. I need to give some things away!

The same can be said of my heart today. I have a clutter of stored hurts and pains. I also have incredible stories of how God's promises have gotten me through. Just as I need to give away some of my material blessings, perhaps I should give away more of my stories of hope. I need to comfort others with the ways God has comforted me.

What hope have you already received from God? Find hope today by looking into your heart of stored comfort and passing along a bit of that comfort to someone God puts on your mind or along your path.

Dear Father, open my eyes to see who needs comfort today. Bring to my mind the story from my past (or present) that will comfort someone else. Then multiply that comfort many times over. Amen.

Day 11

We take captive every thought
to make it obedient to Christ.

—*2 Corinthians 10:5*

When I was little, my parents would listen to a radio program called *Swap & Shop*. People who were tired of their current belongings could call in to offer a swap so they could shop for something new.

Are you tired of your current thoughts? Swap them for something more uplifting. It works this way: First, listen to your thoughts. Which one do you want to swap? That's the one to "take captive." Now, go to your Bible and "shop" for a scripture to replace that old thought. For example, when you think, *I'm so afraid*, swap it with, *God has not given me a spirit of fear, but of a sound mind*. Get the idea?

Day 11

Find hope today by shopping for new truths to replace your own, worn-out lies.

Dear Father, thanks for making Your truths so easy to grasp. Swap and shop. I get that! I'll need Your help, though. Guide me to the right scriptures that will grow my hope, and give me the strength to let go of the lies I've been believing. Amen.

Day 12

Your enemy the devil prowls around
like a roaring lion looking for
someone to devour.

—*1 Peter 5:8*

A lion's roar is intended to intimidate, to make its victim feel threatened, helpless, *hopeless*. But no matter how much your enemy roars, he cannot win. Why? First, you are *not* a victim. Christ, who is in you, is greater than the enemy who is in the world. Second, Satan may be like a lion, but Jesus is your protector. The enemy has no real power over you—never has, never will. The roar—that's all he's got.

Find hope today in knowing that when your enemy comes looking for you today, he'll have to make it past Jesus. And he won't.

Day 12

Dear Father, the enemy may be "like" a lion, but one of Jesus' names is Lion of Judah. Thank You for giving me a Savior who is not a counterfeit lion, but the real deal. Thank You for restoring my hope with Your promise of protection. Amen.

Notes and Reflections

Day 13

Resist him, standing firm in the faith,
because you know that the family
of believers throughout the world is
undergoing the same kind of sufferings.

—*1 Peter 5:9*

Misery loves company, and while I wish no misery on anyone, that old saying comes to my mind each time I read today's passage. Oddly, it makes me feel a bit better.

Haven't you ever thought, *Am I the only one?* Everyone at the mall or in the office looks so together and worry-free. No one else seems to be struggling. This verse says otherwise: everyone around you today—and around the world—is fighting some type of battle. Take comfort in knowing you are not alone. Find hope today in knowing you can resist and stand firm alongside the rest of your family of faith.

Dear Father, You never intended Your children to be alone. When You drew us to Yourself, You drew us into a family. What a gift! Help me to bring hope to my family by being authentic and honest about my struggles so none of us ever feels alone again. Amen.

Day 14

The God of all grace, who called
you to his eternal glory in Christ,
after you have suffered a little while,
will himself restore you and make
you strong, firm and steadfast.

—*1 Peter 5:10*

God doesn't sugarcoat anything. While we
may buy into the myth that accepting Christ
means an easy, problem-free, happy life, that is
just not true.

What is true? That we have an everlasting relationship and an eternal glory in Christ.

Do you find it hard to picture *everlasting* and
eternal? Imagine a dot—your earthly life. From
that dot, begin to draw a line. Continue that line
around the globe … and around the globe again
… and again, again, and again. That line is just

the beginning of eternity and the eternal glory you've been promised.

For now, you may suffer, but it won't always be so. Find hope today in knowing that the God of all grace is—at this moment, even as you struggle—working out His plan for your eternal gain.

Dear Father, I can't grasp eternity, let alone eternity in Your presence. But I know it will be good. Thank You for creating such an amazing plan for my life, which is also eternal. Wow and amen!

Day 15

I, the LORD, …
will take hold of your hand.

—*Isaiah 42:6*

Among my favorite childhood memories are my walks with Daddy. My little arm could barely reach and hold on to the big hand he extended to me. But the security, the sense of belonging, and the pure joy it brought kept me holding on long after my arm had fallen numb. That's the image that comes to my mind as I read today's passage. And with God, I don't have to hold on because His hand is holding on to me.

Do you have a memory of a time when you felt thoroughly loved and secure? If not, ponder your longing for this kind of love. Let that be a starting place for your belief in God's love for you to grow. I say "starting place" because God's love so surpasses even the best human love such that no earthbound memory or longing can quite capture it. Find hope today in knowing your Father's love will always exceed your wildest expectations.

Dear Father, I'm trying to imagine how it would feel to have my small hand in Yours. Break through my shell, and let me sense Your love today. Amen.

Notes and Reflections

Day 16

I came that they may have life
and have it abundantly.
—*John 10:10 ESV*

We all have dreams, don't we? We all feel there is more inside of us yet to be discovered. Do you dream of having more confidence? Of being able to transform a blank sheet of paper into a bestseller? Of finding a place to fit in? Our dreams are as unique and varied as we are.

But when our dreams remain out of reach, we lose hope, don't we? We ditch the piano lessons, drop the workout sessions, and settle for what's more attainable. There's another way, however, of looking at unrealized dreams. They could be God's whispered invitation to move beyond our small dreams and into His big dream for us. Even when we find ourselves in good places in life, God is always inviting us to more, to *abundance*.

Don't stop dreaming! Find hope today by surrendering to God's dream for you—and believing it is beyond anything you could have imagined.

Dear Father, have I been dreaming too small? Show me Your dreams for me. Rekindle my hope that life can have meaning and purpose. Amen.

Day 17

Do you not know? Have you not heard?
The LORD is the everlasting God,
the Creator of the ends of the earth.

—*Isaiah 40:28*

When life becomes twisted and tangled, we may start to believe that God is as befuddled and helpless as we are. In truth, with a mere flick of His hand, He sets kings on thrones and removes them, heals tumors, restores incomes, mends marriages, and so much more. No matter what is happening (or not happening) in your life, and no matter how hard you struggle and strive to set things right, in the end you need to call upon the Creator of all things, *your* Creator. He alone knows how to take all the messy, broken pieces and put them back together as they were created to be.

Day 17

Whatever you face, find hope today in knowing that your powerful Creator can set things right.

Dear Father, I am so sorry for forgetting that nothing is too hard for You. You are greater than my mind can grasp. You created me, and You know exactly how to put me back together again when I'm helpless and hopeless. All I can say is thank You. Amen.

Day 18

I know that you can do all things;
no purpose of yours can be thwarted.

—*Job 42:2*

Job, a man besieged by troubles and trials, made the above declaration *in the midst of* his suffering. Not after everything was resolved. In the midst of it.

Everyone is dealing with hard stuff. Everyone. Everyone needs someone to believe in, someone who can handle the personal worries and the big "what's this world coming to" worries. God is that someone. You know it in your head and heart. But when hope is in short supply, do you send a different message?

Be like Job today. In the midst of your trials, announce the truth about God. He can do anything. No purpose of His can be thwarted. Find hope today by being a hope giver who tells the truth about God.

Dear Father, I'm afraid I let my lack of hope bring others down. Today, help me to change all that. Use me to give hope to others. Amen.

Notes and Reflections

Day 19

God chose the weak things of the world.

—*1 Corinthians 1:27*

Have you ever thought, *My life is nothing to brag about?* That's great! You're exactly the kind of person God is looking for.

We mistakenly think God can only use the good stuff in our lives. Because we do not have a flawless past, we are convinced we have nothing to offer Him. We lose hope.

God can and does use our successes, talents, and gifts, but He also uses our hurts and burdens for His good purposes. In fact, it's most often our pain that people can relate to and where they find hope. Right now, offer the junk in your life to God—the flaws, mistakes, sin, foolishness, weaknesses. Find hope today in knowing He can transform them in ways you cannot imagine.

Day 19

Dear Father, my offering to you today is all the messes I've made. I'm stunned to think that's what You want to use to bring hope to others, and I'm humbled. Thank You for transforming my junk into beauty. Amen.

Day 20

When I am weak,
then I am strong.
—*2 Corinthians 12:10*

I have a whimsical towel hanging in my kitchen that reads, "It's exhausting being this perfect!" While intended to be lighthearted, that quip accurately describes the heaviness I felt from years of living behind a wardrobe of masks so no one would know how far short of perfection I was. But the apostle Paul knew what I had yet to learn: "When I am weak, then I am strong."

Perfectionism is one of the mightiest hope killers I know. But God removed the burden of perfection from you. Because of the grace of Christ on the cross, perfection is His job, not yours. Find hope today in knowing God loves you just as you are. No perfection required.

Day 20

Dear Father, thank You for letting Your perfect Son die on a cross to free me from the burden of being perfect on my own. My hope soars when I realize how much You love me and what a huge price You paid to make me Your own. I love You, Lord. Amen.

Day 21

There is a time for everything.

—*Ecclesiastes 3:1*

While visiting my freshman son at college some years ago, I could see his disappointment. He had failed to earn a starting position on the football team. With wisdom and understanding, his coach said to me, "Your son has great potential. He is going to have a great career. But for now, he is right where he needs to be."

May I pass along that coach's encouragement and hope to you? You are right where you need to be. Sometimes God may move faster than you want. At other times, He may seem to take forever. But find hope today in this unchanging truth: His timing is always perfect.

Day 21

Dear Father, sometimes I feel forgotten, sidelined. I wonder if You see any potential in me. Thank You for reminding me that Your timing is perfect and so is Your love for me. I will wait on You with hope. Amen.

Notes and Reflections

Day 22

Your word is a lamp for my feet,
a light on my path.

—*Psalm 119:105*

At a point in my journey toward hope, when darkness seemed to be prevailing, I came upon this verse. I slowly grew to understand that God's truth shines light onto the path, but I have to choose to walk that path. I can't just stand there and admire it.

Does that sound daunting to you? Look at it this way: God could just point to the path and let you stumble along as best you can. But He won't. He not only prepared a path for you, but He also prepared a light to guide you on that path. The light is His Word, your Bible. Find hope today in this amazing gift and in the Father's love behind the gift.

Dear Father, sometimes when I lose hope, I also lose sight of the gift of Your Word. Thanks for reminding me today of the riches I can find there. I'm not in the dark after all. I follow a well-lit path toward a future I can trust because it's Your future for me. Amen.

Day 23

Therefore, since we are surrounded
by such a great cloud of witnesses …

—*Hebrews 12:1*

The Bible is filled with stories from that "cloud of witnesses," people who accomplished great things. One reason those stories are there, I believe, is to renew our hope when it falters. We are reminded that we too can become who God created us to be and accomplish what He wants us to do. I turn regularly to these stories so my hope can stay strong.

God designed us to be inspired by the lives of others. Set aside a few minutes today to read Hebrews 11. If you meet someone there whom you'd like to get to know better, use your Bible's index (or concordance) to seek out their full story. Find hope today in reading about others who held on to hope in the direst of circumstances.

Dear Father, thank You for understanding my need for inspiration. Sometimes I try too hard and too long to go it alone. I'm eager to read about others who stayed strong and faithful against all hope. Amen.

Day 24

All things are possible with God.
—*Mark 10:27*

God wants to work in your life in ways that may seem impossible to you but are a cinch for the God of the universe. It is a lie to think you are too messed up or it is too late to be a part of His plan for you. With God, nothing is impossible.

All those repulsive, hurtful bits of you that shout condescending little messages—they don't intimidate Him. All the mistakes, hurts, and abandoned dreams—He wades right on through, proclaiming, "I can work with that!" What you or others may deem spiritually catastrophic, God stands ready and able to put to use. I'll say it again: with God, nothing is impossible.

Day 24

You may be on the verge of becoming God's greatest miracle. Find hope today by believing He can reverse your burdens to blessings.

Dear Father, today I choose to let You work through me, providing the faith and strength I need to believe the impossible is possible. Your words give me hope, and I want to share that hope with others as well. Please use me. Amen.

Notes and Reflections

Day 25

We do not know what to do,
but our eyes are on you.
—*2 Chronicles 20:12*

Racehorses are easily distracted by what's beside them. That's where blinders come in. Blinders are leather flaps attached to a horse's bridle to prevent sideways vision. They keep a horse's focus solely on what lies ahead—the finish line.

What is distracting you today and stealing your hope? Regret, worry, fear, doubt? Anger? A troubled relationship? Health challenges? A task bigger than your capacity? Try putting on your spiritual blinders. You may feel helpless and hopeless, but when you keep your eyes focused solely upon God, you find fresh energy to run the race, win the battle, seize the day, or any other analogy you want to use! Find hope today by turning your focus onto God alone.

Dear Father, when I focus on You, I see that You have everything I need to meet any challenge. I see that You are loving, powerful, merciful, strong, just, gracious, sovereign, and so much more. Today, when my focus strays, please bring it back to You. Amen.

Day 26

Those who hope in the Lord
will renew their strength.
They will soar on wings like eagles.

—*Isaiah 40:31*

When hope is weak, we tend to flap our wings a lot. Have you noticed that? Isaiah tells us that when our hope is properly focused, we will soar like eagles.

Soaring eagles rely on updrafts to lift them high, help them glide (no flapping required), and give them a wider perspective. When you've lost hope, isn't a wider perspective what you long for? It is for me! Weariness comes when every ounce of our strength is so focused on the hope-robbing circumstance or person or memory that we can't see anything else. We desperately need a bird's-eye view that sees and believes that God is good and in control.

Find hope today in knowing that God lifts the perspective of those who call on Him.

Dear Father, please help me. I want to soar like an eagle. I'm so tired of flapping. And I'm weary from fixating on my hope robber. Lift me on the updraft of Your love and open my eyes to a wider perspective of what You are doing in and through me. Amen.

Day 27

Yes, my soul, find rest in God;
my hope comes from him.

—*Psalm 62:5*

The moment I lie down to sleep, I begin to wrestle with tomorrow. Are you like that too? A multitude of "what ifs" haunt me. I rehearse the day's anticipated events and imagine every possible worst-case scenario.

The psalmist says, "Find rest in God." Maybe we should all carve those words in the headboards of our beds! Or maybe we should end each day by praying, "Good night, Lord. I leave tomorrow in Your sovereign hands." Many nights you won't want to pray those words. But keep praying them anyway. You'll enjoy much better sleep. And you'll find hope today in knowing that tomorrow is already taken care of by God alone.

Day 27

Dear Father, thanks for being the Giver of rest. I'm sorry for being so forgetful, for thinking it's up to me to work out every detail of tomorrow, for trying to control every contingency. Only You know the future; only You can work out the details. My role is to rest and enjoy the gift of hope that You offer. Help me to do that. Amen.

Notes and Reflections

Day 28

I thank my God every time
I remember you.
—*Philippians 1:3*

The biggest robbers of our hope can be people. Do I hear an amen? But get this: the biggest *givers* of hope can also be people. The problem is they're often the people we don't pay much attention to.

Challenge yourself to notice the hope givers in your life today. The barista who gives you a big smile at the coffee shop. The driver who waves you over when you're stuck in the wrong traffic lane. The men who pick up your trash (imagine if they didn't show up each week!). When I walk through my day with this perspective, I begin to see brief yet beautiful twinkles of light all around me, like lightning bugs on a summer night. Find hope today in taking the time to notice those who bring light into your life.

Dear Father, thank You for filling my days with these tiny bursts of hope. Help me to be a hope giver to others as well. Amen.

Day 29

The LORD blessed the latter part of Job's life
more than the former part.

—Job 42:12

Just when we're about to lose hope, Job's life
reminds us to expect God to do good things.

Job loved God and obeyed Him. Yet he lost
everything. How easily he could have declared
God's unfairness or demanded to know, "Why
me?" But rather than choosing bitterness or giving up hope, Job chose to get up every morning
and do what he knew God wanted him to do that
day. His conduct sent the message, "No matter
my circumstances, I have hope in God." In the
end, God not only turned around Job's calamity,
He also restored to Job twice what he had had in
the beginning.

What seems unfair to you? Hopeless? Find

hope today in Job's example and in God's promised restoration in your life.

Dear Father, as hopeless as I feel sometimes, I've never lost all that Job lost. But parts of me are worn down by hurt and disappointment and loss. Restore my life, Lord. And while I wait, help me to model hope and trust like Job did. Amen.

Day 30

He calls his own sheep
by name.
—*John 10:3*

God sees you today. He knows you personally and intimately. From among any crowd, He can pick you out and call you by name.

How can you be sure of this? Because the Good Shepherd, described in today's verse, is also your heavenly Father who created you, loves you, and knows the real you. If you are feeling misplaced at work, reeling from an argument that has left you isolated, or feeling abandoned because your prayers remain unanswered, be assured: you are not forgotten. Your Shepherd sees you. He whispers, "Just stay still. I know exactly where you are, and I'm on My way to get you."

You may feel forgotten sometimes, but you never are. Find hope today in God's constant, caring awareness of you.

Dear Father, thank You that neither I nor my circumstances are forgotten by You. I'm sure a lot of people today feel forgotten. Help me to notice them and reach out to them with this message of hope. Amen.

Notes and Reflections

Day 31

And God said,
"Let there be light."
—*Genesis 1:3*

Darkness is a fact of life this side of heaven. Our hope, however, lies in this deep truth: God has been interrupting the darkness since the beginning of time. He will keep interrupting yours as well. Find hope today in writing your own prayer to God, thanking Him for shining on your life and giving you renewed hope for the days ahead.

Day 31

May the God of hope fill you
with all joy and peace as you trust in him,
so that you may overflow with hope
by the power of the Holy Spirit.

—*Romans 15:13*

Notes and Reflections

About the Author

Kim is the founder and president of Roses and Rainbows Ministries, Inc., and Community COFFEEs (Conversations of Friends of Faith to Encourage and Equip). She has traveled nationally for more than twenty years—speaking at retreats, conferences, and to Bible study groups—and has been interviewed on national TV and radio.

Kim's message and passion come from her personal experience of longing to be used by God yet feeling unusable because of past abuse, anorexia, diet-pill addiction, and depression. Her mother's deathbed challenge set Kim on the path of daring to be and do what God had purposed for her, a journey she wrote about in her book *Burdens to Blessings*. She is also author of *Infinitely More* and *A Cup of Christmas: 31 Daily Readings for December*.

Kim is married to Lee Crabill, and together they have two sons.

For more information about Kim Crabill and her ministries, visit www.rosesandrainbows.org.